MAYAN CIVILIZATION

THE HISTORY DETECTIVE INVESTIGATES

THE HISTORY DETECTIVE INVESTIGATES

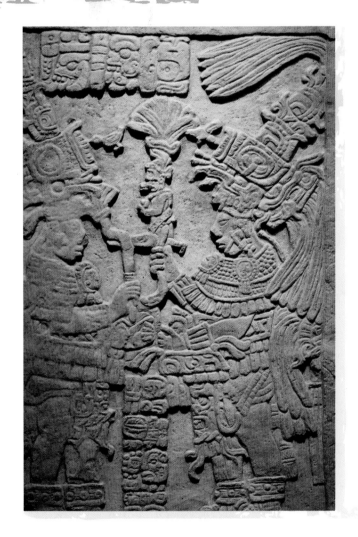

Clare Hibbert

WAYLAND

First published in 2014 by Wayland

Copyright © Wayland 2014

Wayland
338 Euston Road
London NW1 3BH

Wayland Australia
Level 17/207 Kent Street
Sydney, NSW 2000

The History Detective Investigates series:

Produced for Wayland by
White-Thomson Publishing Ltd
www.wtpub.co.uk
+44 (0)843 208 7460

Editor: Clare Hibbert
Designer: Ian Winton
Cover design concept: Lisa Peacock
Consultant: Philip Parker
Proofreader: Lucy Ross

A catalogue record for this title is available from the British Library.

ISBN: 978-0-7502-8176-8
eBook ISBN: 978-0-7502-8538-4

Dewey Number: 972.8'1016-dc23

Printed in Malaysia

10 9 8 7 6 5 4 3 2 1

Wayland is a division of Hachette Children's Books, an Hachette UK company

Picture Acknowledgments: Stefan Chabluk: 5t; **Corbis:** 27t; **Dreamstime:** 1 (Coplandj), 6l (Jctabb), 14 (Hugoht), 19l (Alexandre Fagundes De Fagundes), 26 (Christian Delbert); **Shutterstock:** cover b (rui vale sousa), folios (Vojtech Vlk), 4 (My Nguyen), 9t (Ragne Kabanova), 9b (ventdusud), 15r (Victor Torres), 17t (Milagli), 20r (Jorge R. Gonzalez), 21 (Irafael), 22 (Kim Briers), 25 (worldswildlifewonders), 27b (Patryk Kosmider), 28 (Cyril Papot); **TopFoto:** 16 (World History Archive), 18 (Ann Ronan Picture Library/Heritage Images), 24r (Werner Forman Archive/David Bernstein, New York); **Werner Forman Archive:** 2 (Private Collection), 10t (British Museum), 11 (National Museum of Anthropology, Mexico), 13t, 13b (Private Collection, New York), 17b (David Bernstein, New York), 19r (National Museum of Anthropology, Mexico), 20l (National Museum of Anthropology, Mexico), 23t (Edward H. Merrin Gallery, New York), 24l (David Bernstein, New York), 29l (Private Collection, New York); **Wikimedia:** cover t (Michel wal), 5c (Michel wal), 6r (Daderot), 7 (Simon Burchell), 8 (Aiwok), 10b (Wolfgang Saube), 12 (Daderot), 15l (BabelStone), 23b (Jacob Rus), 29r (Jami Dwyer/National Museum of Anthropology).

Above: An **obsidian** knife used in Mayan rituals, carved into the shape of the god of lightning.

Previous page: A carved limestone **lintel** found at Yaxchilan, Mexico, dating to around 750 CE.

Cover (top): Page from a replica of one of four surviving Mayan books, the Madrid **Codex**.

Cover (bottom): The Temple of Kukulcan, the feathered serpent god, at Chichén Itzá, Mexico.

CONTENTS

Words in **bold** can be found in the glossary on page 30.

The history detective Sherlock Bones will help you to find clues and collect evidence about the Maya. Wherever you see one of Sherlock's paw-prints, you will find a mystery to solve. The answers are on page 31.

WHO WERE THE MAYA?

The Maya were people who lived in the forests of Central America. Their civilization was at its height from around 250 until 900 CE. During this time, which is known as the Classic period, the Maya established powerful city-states. Their society was complex, and the people had organized religion, writing and impressive architecture.

The Maya's ancestors had crossed to North America from Asia more than 20,000 years ago and then gradually moved south. They reached Central America about 12,000 years ago. Between 5000 and 2000 BCE, the Maya changed their lifestyle. They went from living as hunters on the move to settling down in villages, as farmers.

Historians call the period in Mayan history from 2000 BCE to 250 CE the Preclassic. During this time, the Maya developed complex religious beliefs and erected monumental temples. They came up with their system of writing and built their first cities. El Mirador was inhabited from the 500s BCE and may have had over 100,000 inhabitants. It contains one of the earliest and largest Mayan **pyramids**: known as the La Danta temple, it stands 70 m (230 ft) high. Tikal was also founded in the Preclassic period, although the city was most powerful in the 700s CE. Like other **city-states** of the Classic period, Tikal was ruled by a **dynasty** of kings.

DETECTIVE WORK

Visit http://mayas.mrdonn.org/games.html for interactive games about Mayan civilization.

David Stuart, an expert in Mayan hieroglyphics, describes visiting Tikal:

'It's the atmosphere of the place. Tikal is simply one of the most overpowering archaeological sites in the world.'

These are the ruins of Tikal in Guatemala. Its population may have reached 90,000, with nearly half a million more living in the surrounding area.

Mayan lands included much of modern-day Mexico and Guatemala, all of Belize, and parts of Honduras and El Salvador.

▼ This plaque of a Mayan king was discovered at Teotihuacán. It proves that there was contact between the Teotihuacános and the Maya.

Around 900 CE, Tikal, Copán, Palenque and the other great Mayan cities were abandoned. **Archaeologists** are still not entirely sure why, although there are many theories. Nevertheless, Mayan culture continued in the Postclassic period (900-1500 CE) in the uplands of the Yucatán in Mexico, for example at Uxmal and Chichén Itzá.

The region where the Maya and others developed advanced civilizations is called **Mesoamerica**. Peoples included the Olmecs, Teotihuacános and Aztecs. Further south, in the Andes of Peru, the Incas established a mighty but short-lived empire. All of these cultures came to an end with the arrival of Spanish explorers in the 1500s (see pages 26-27).

🐾 **What is unusual about the ear of the king on the jade plaque?**

Several civilizations rose and fell in Mesoamerica at the same time as the Maya.

People	Flourished	Key centres
Olmecs	1500-300 BCE	San Lorenzo, La Venta
Teotihuacános	200 BCE-700 CE	Teotihuacán
Zapotecs	1500 BCE-700 CE	Monte Albán
Mixtecs	900-1450 CE	Tilantongo, Monte Albán
Toltecs	900-1200 CE	Tula, Chichén Itzá
Aztecs	1325-1521 CE	Tenochtitlán

WHAT DID MAYAN FARMERS GROW?

Around 4250 BCE, the Maya began to cultivate maize. Before then, they had lived as hunter-gatherers, hunting animals for meat and gathering roots, seeds and fruit. Hunter-gatherers lived on the move. Once they took up farming, the Maya began to establish settled villages.

Mayan farmers cleared fields in the rainforest using stone axes. Once they had chopped down most of the trees, they set fire to the remaining plant growth. This technique, called **slash-and-burn**, produced ash to fertilize the soil. However, nutrients soon washed away because heavy rain fell most days. The Maya learned to give the land time to recover. They also built terraces in upland areas to stop the soil slipping downhill, and in drier places they dug channels to irrigate (water) the land. Success at farming meant a stable food supply, and made it possible for city-states to develop. No wonder the Maya worshipped maize as a god!

Dating to around 700 CE, this vase shows the maize deity dancing. According to some beliefs, he was a version of the creator god, Itzamna (see page 12).

Mayan farmers gradually achieved better maize harvests by selecting seeds from the plumpest corncobs.

Besides maize, the Maya planted beans, squash, peppers, sweet potatoes, tomatoes and cassava (a plant with a starchy root). They gathered cacao beans from wild trees and grew breadnut, avocado and papaya trees. They even kept bees for honey. Maize was their most important crop, though. It provided people's daily bread. Flatbread accompanied every meal and was baked on a stone over an open fire. Maize was also turned into porridge, or fermented to make an alcoholic drink.

This is a Mayan grinding stone or _metate_. Its flat surface was used to mash soggy corn kernels into a dough that could be rolled out to make flatbread.

The Maya continued to hunt deer, peccaries (pig-like animals) and tapirs in the forest but they also domesticated turkeys and dogs and kept them for food. Not all dogs were for eating. Some helped with hunting, while others were fattened up to be sacrificed (see pages 12-15).

🐾 **What meat did the Maya eat?**

The Maya prized cacao beans, both for use as money and also to make a bitter chocolate drink, which they sometimes spiced with chilli. In their 2005 book about chocolate, David Wolfe and Shazzie wrote:

'_Chocolate to the Mayans and Aztecs was referred to as_ yollotl eztli _(heart blood)…_'

DETECTIVE WORK

Find out more about the history of chocolate here: www.historyforkids.org/ learn/food/chocolate.htm

HOW MANY CITY-STATES WERE THERE?

There was never one single Mayan nation. The Maya developed more than sixty separate city-states, which had their own kings but shared the same culture, language and beliefs. These city-states were mostly independent from each other, although smaller ones sometimes came under the control of larger, more powerful ones.

Archaeologists have uncovered the remains of many settlements, scattered mostly across Guatemala and Mexico. The best-known include Tikal, Calakmul, Palenque, Caracol, Copán and Yaxchilan. Mayan merchants travelled between these cities (see pages 24-25), some of which were even connected by roads, but not all contact was friendly. Violent struggles for power and resources kept certain city-states at war for years. Tikal and Calakmul were two of the bitterest rivals.

This lintel carving shows victorious Bird Jaguar IV of Yaxchilan with a captive from a rival city-state in 752 CE.

DETECTIVE WORK

Find out about the geography of the different city-states here: http://www.smm.org/sln/ma/sites.html

The nineteenth-century U.S. explorer John Lloyd Stephens described seeing Mayan monuments for the first time:

'...standing as they do in the depths of a tropical forest, silent and solemn, strange in design, excellent in sculpture, rich in ornament, different from the works of any other people, their uses and purposes and whole history so entirely unknown with hieroglyphics explaining all, but being perfectly unintelligible...'

What is Bird Jaguar holding in his right hand?

Many Mesoamerican cultures built cities according to a formal grid or plan that was meant to represent the order of the universe. Teotihuacán, with its broad central avenue, was one example. Mayan cities were not planned. Built in stages over decades or even centuries, they developed in a higgledy-piggledy fashion. The city centre was packed with impressive pyramids, temples and palaces, which housed the royal family and religious leaders. Nearby were the administrative buildings used by the civil service, and the ball courts – ritual ball games were a feature of life in all Mesoamerican cultures.

Just 2.5 sq km (one sq mi) of the city of Palenque has been excavated. The rest is still covered by rainforest.

Residences belonging to the **elite** class were close to the centre. Built from limestone, they stood on mounds or platforms of earth and stone to avoid any risk of flooding. There were stone walkways linking different mounds. Houses were often built as part of bigger complexes, where buildings belonged to other members of the same family. This meant that people could live alongside their relatives. Sometimes they shared certain spaces within the complex, such as the garden or kitchen area. Further from the city centre there were more modest homes. They were simply constructed from lashed-together wooden poles. The roof was thatched with palms to help the rain run off. On the edge of the city were the farmers' homes and fields.

This reconstruction of a traditional Mayan house stands at Chichén Itzá.

WHO RULED THE MAYA?

All-powerful kings – or occasionally queens – ruled over the city-states. Many of them showed their importance by building awe-inspiring temples or pyramids. People worshipped their kings and queens like gods. Rulers had to perform specific rituals to protect their subjects and bring them prosperity. In times of war, they commanded the city-state's fighting forces.

This is a section of a panel depicting twenty kings of Copán – Yax Pac, the city's final ruler, and his nineteen predecessors, back from the afterlife to attend his coronation.

Mayan writings record the rulers in most city-states and the dates of their reigns. Archaeologists can name the seventeen rulers of Palenque from 431 CE until the city was abandoned around 800. The most famous was Pakal I, also known as Pakal the Great, who ruled from 615 to 683 CE. He ordered the construction of some of Palenque's finest buildings and founded a great dynasty. He was only twelve when he became king, and his mother Sak Tuk wielded a lot of power in the early years of his reign – she may even have been queen.

Alberto Ruz, director of research at Palenque, describes discovering the tomb of Pakal in 1952:

'Out of the dim shadows emerged a vision from a fairy tale, a fantastic, ethereal sight from another world. It seemed a huge magic grotto carved out of ice… an abandoned chapel.'

This stunning jade funeral mask belonged to Pakal the Great.

What is Pakal the Great's funeral mask carved from?

Mayan princes had to prepare for kingship. Aged five or six, they had their first **bloodletting** (see page 15). Later, they went off to war to prove their bravery in battle. When the existing ruler died or gave up the throne, the heir was made king at a special ceremony where he had to hold a sceptre, wear a headdress of **quetzal** feathers and sit on a jaguar skin. As ruler, he had many religious duties to carry out. The king had to be the link between his people and the gods. He also had to welcome visitors from other city-states and entertain them.

The king was at the top of Mayan society, along with his wives and children. They were closely followed by the elite, who were mostly royal relatives. The city-state's **administrators**, generals, scribes and priests were part of the elite. Architects, craftspeople, merchants and warriors all had a respectable role in society. Next came the farmers and labourers. Finally, at the bottom of the heap, were the slaves. Usually captured in warfare from other city-states, slaves did back-breaking building work or were given as sacrifices to the gods.

DETECTIVE WORK

Find lists of Mayan rulers here: http://www. ancientworlds.net/aw/ Article/897005

This painted pottery figure shows a Mayan nobleman. A member of the elite, he helped to run the state.

WHO WERE THE MAYAN GODS?

The Maya had a rich mythology and worshipped many gods. At least thirty are recorded by name, but there were plenty more. Some deities took human form, others were animals and some could shift between different forms and identities. Gods rose and fell in terms of importance, but the supreme one was usually Itzamna.

Itzamna was the Mayan creator god. Lord of day and night and ruler of the heavens, he was said to have made humankind and devised its religious rituals, writing and calendar. Itzamna was often depicted as a toothless old man with a crooked nose. His wife Ixchel was goddess of childbirth, healing, weaving and the moon. Girls made offerings to her before they married. Ixchel was sometimes shown with jaguar ears or claws and wore a headdress with a snake curled around it. She might also have been the storm goddess, able to wreak havoc by bringing devastating floods.

Many deities looked after the weather and crops, which were vital to Mayan survival. Chac, the rain god, was a gentle warrior, who watered the crops with his tears. The sun god, Kinich-Ahau, crossed the sky each day bringing warmth and light, but at night he took the form of a jaguar and turned into the fearsome god of darkness. Skull-headed Ah Puch was associated with death. The Maya believed he entered people's homes after dark and stole their souls. Tohil was the terrible god of fire and sacrifice. At Chichén Itzá, people worshipped Kukulcan, the feathered serpent. Similar deities occur in other Mesoamerican cultures – the Aztec version was Quetzalcoatl, god of knowledge.

DETECTIVE WORK

Visit this website for an introduction to Mayan deities and an A–Z list of their names: http://www.godchecker.com/pantheon/mayan-mythology.php

The sun god Kinich-Ahau could appear as an old or a young man, and usually had an extremely large nose.

Thousands of Mayan manuscripts describing their beliefs were destroyed by the sixteenth-century Spanish bishop Diego de Landa (see page 27), who wrote:

'*We found a large number of these books … and, as they contained nothing in which there was not to be seen superstition and lies of the devil, we burned them all, which [the Maya] regretted to an amazing degree and which caused them great affliction.*'

This stone wall at Uxmal has been carved to show the face of Chac, the rain god. He was the son of Itzamna and Ixchel.

Discovered at Palenque, this terracotta incense burner shows a priest or possibly the sun god.

The main source of information about Mayan myths is a book called the *Popol Vuh*. It tells of cunning Hunahpu and Xbalanque, twin sons of the maize god, Hun Hunahpu. The Hero Twins famously outwitted the gods of the underworld in a ball game (see page 15). The *Popol Vuh* also describes the Mayan view of the universe. They believed it was made up of three layers – the underworld, the earth and the upper realm, which was held up by Pauahtun, the drunken god of thunder and wind.

🐾 **On the incense burner, what is beneath the priest's feet?**

WHY DID THE MAYA BUILD PYRAMIDS?

Tall, stepped pyramids were built to support Mayan temples, holding them as close to the upper realm as possible. Reaching into the skies, pyramids were a link to the gods. Some were also used as tombs, holding the remains of dead rulers in chambers deep within them.

Building pyramids was quite a feat. First, labourers piled up the central core of earth and rubble. Then they faced it with blocks of limestone, stuck together with a kind of plaster. The Maya did not have wheeled vehicles or draft animals. They transported all the huge blocks of limestone from their quarries on log rollers.

Pyramid-top temples were the site of public ceremonies, carried out to keep the gods happy. Crowds of spectators gathered far below, craning their necks to see what was going on. Only rulers, priests and, of course, sacrificial victims, were allowed to climb the pyramid steps. The Maya believed that their gods needed offerings of blood. One way to supply this was by sacrificing slaves, who were usually prisoners-of-war. Victims were beheaded with an axe or, in the Postclassic period, had their heart cut out while it was still beating.

DETECTIVE WORK

Take a tour of the pyramids at Chichén Itzá here: video. nationalgeographic.co.uk/ video/specials/ancient-mysteries/chichen-itza-temples/

The Temple of the Inscriptions stood on top of the largest pyramid at Palenque, shown here in the foreground. Inside was the tomb of Pakal the Great.

Another ritual was bloodletting, carried out upon kings and members of the elite. To make the person bleed, a spine from a stingray fish was used to pierce their tongue, lips or ears, or they were simply cut with a stone knife. The Maya believed that the visions caused by the blood loss brought them closer to their ancestors and the gods. Bloodletting was an honour.

In his book *Relación de las Cosas de Yucatán*, Diego de Landa described Mayan blood sacrifices:

'*They offered sacrifices of their own blood … they pierced their tongues in a slanting direction from side to side and passed bits of straw through the holes with horrible suffering…*'

🐾 **What was the name of Shield Jaguar's queen?**

◀ **Shield Jaguar the Great, King of Yaxchilan, performs a bloodletting ritual on his kneeling wife, Lady K'ab'al Xook.**

Ball courts were religious places, too. Here, players re-enacted the exploits of the Hero Twins (see page 13). According to the story, the twins had irritated the gods with their noisy ball playing. They had to go through a series of trials that ended with the gods knocking off Hunahpu's head to use as a ball. Quick-thinking Xbalanque managed to whack the head-ball out of the court and reattach it to his brother's neck. In real ball games, the two teams passed the rubber ball around without using their hands. Some experts believe that the winners were rewarded with death – a sure and quick route to the afterlife; others think the losing team was killed. A third theory is that the audience gave up their clothes to the winners if they won by striking the ball through the hoop!

Ball players tried to pass the ball through the stone hoops high on the ball court walls.

WHAT WAS MAYAN WRITING LIKE?

The Maya used symbols called hieroglyphs to write things down. These were painted on to bark paper, wood or pottery, or carved into stone. The earliest examples of Mayan writing are stone inscriptions that date to the 200s BCE – nearly 500 years before the Classic period of Mayan history began.

People who study inscriptions and hieroglyphs are called epigraphers. So far, epigraphers know of around 1,100 Mayan **hieroglyphs**. These were usually read from left to right in a row and then top to bottom in a column. Some represented whole words or groups of words – that is, they stood for actual objects or ideas. Some represented sounds just as our letters of the alphabet do. Others were more like punctuation – they acted as signposts in the block to indicate how the hieroglyphs should be read and which were the most important.

Language expert Barbara MacLeod has taught herself to speak ancient Mayan:

'We can only make guesses as to how those Maya languages actually sounded, but we base them on performance characteristics of the modern languages, so I think we can get a pretty good idea.'

DETECTIVE WORK

Watch a programme all about deciphering Mayan writing: www.pbs.org/wgbh/nova/ancient/cracking-maya-code.html

The Troano Codex is a Mayan manuscript dating to the 1400s. The paper was made from fig tree bark.

The Maya developed their own number system and a way of writing numbers down. They used just three symbols: a shell to mean 'zero', a dot for 'one' and a horizontal line to represent 'five'. Three dots meant 'three', for example, while three lines meant '15'. Today, most cultures use a positional base-ten number system. From right to left numerals represent units between zero and nine, then the quantity of tens, hundreds, thousands, tens of thousands and so on. The Mayan positional number system was base-20, written from bottom to top. The bottom numeral was the number of units between zero and 19, the next indicated how many 20s, then 400s, then 8,000s, then 160,000s and so on.

Using only shells, dots and lines, the Maya could represent any number.

0	1	2	3	4	5	6
7	8	9	10	11	12	13
14	15	16	17	18	19	20

Scribes were members of the elite. They not only recorded events but also read sacred texts in order to advise the king. They probably passed on a basic knowledge of hieroglyphs and numbers to less important officials. Even commoners may have known enough to recognize the glyphs for the king's name and to understand some written numbers.

What animal is the creator god on the relief carving holding in his hand?

The god Itzamna, shown here on a limestone carving, gave the Maya the gift of writing.

WHY DID THE MAYA STARGAZE?

Mayan astronomers observed the movements of the Sun, Moon, Venus and the stars. Knowledge of these heavenly bodies helped the Maya to plan when to plant and harvest their crops, when to practise certain rituals and even when to fight wars. They never discovered that the Sun (not the Earth) is at the centre of the Solar System, but Mayan astronomers were able to predict equinoxes, solstices and eclipses.

The Maya recorded their astronomical observations in two calendars: the 260-day sacred calendar called the *tzolk'in* and the 365-day solar *haab*. The *tzolk'in* consisted of thirteen 20-day periods. Each day was represented by a particular animal, plant or natural force and had its own hieroglyph. The *haab* was made up of eighteen 20-day periods plus a final period of five days, which were considered unlucky. The Maya also recognized a period of time that they called a *baktun*, which amounted to just over 394 solar years.

🐾 **What is the feathered serpent god carrying in the bottom left section of the codex?**

DETECTIVE WORK

Find out more about Mayan calendars here:
http://www.mayankids.com/mmkbeliefs/
calendar.htm

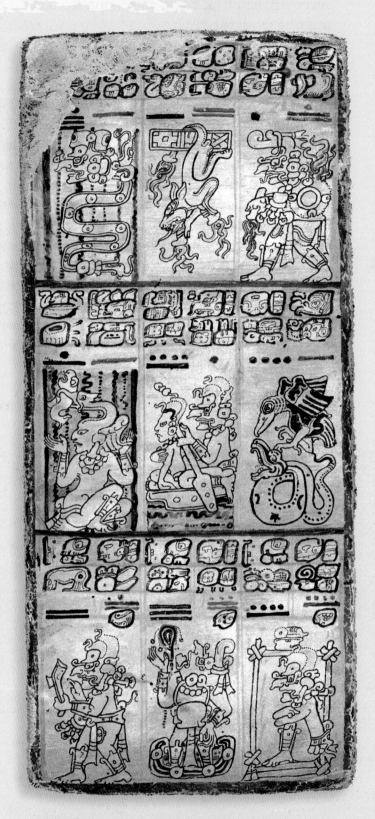

This Mayan codex describes days from the ritual calendar or *tzolk'in*.

The two Mayan calendars interconnected so that every day had two name dates, one from the *haab* and one from the *tzolk'in*. Every fifty-two years, the calendars synched again – in other words, the first days of the *tzolk'in* and *haab* coincided.

The Maya used their knowledge of astronomy when planning their architecture. The circular building at Chichén Itzá known as El Caracol was positioned to line up with various important astronomical events, including equinoxes, solstices, eclipses and the path of the planet Venus. For example, the tower's windows and doors give views of Venus as it appears in the east and then disappears in the west, a cycle that takes 584 days. Five of these cycles took the same amount of time as eight of the Maya's solar years. The planet was also important to the Maya because it was associated with war. Generals timed their battles to coincide with when Venus was in a particular 'lucky' position in the sky.

▶ **The glyphs on this limestone block record a date: 11 February 526 CE in our calendar.**

Climate historian David Hodell of the University of Florida believes the Maya had a good reason to study the sun as it was responsible for a cycle of droughts:

'It looks like changes in the sun's energy output [had] a direct effect on the climate of the Yucatán and [caused] the recurrence of drought, which … in turn influence[d] the Maya evolution.'

El Caracol at Chichén Itzá was probably some kind of observatory, from which Mayan astronomers studied the night sky.

HOW DID THE MAYA DRESS?

Commoners and slaves wore plain loincloths, but the elite added feathers, animal skins or gems as signs of status. Noblemen covered their lower half with a colourful garment that was a cross between a loincloth and a kilt, and often wrapped a square cloak around their shoulders. Women dressed in a skirt and tunic.

Mayan clothes were made from bark cloth, hemp or cotton. Women coloured the yarn first with plant or animal dyes, then wove it into cloth on a simple back-strap loom. This sort of loom has two sticks with the **warp strings** stretched between them, and one of these sticks straps behind the weaver so she can increase the tension in the strings just by leaning back. Looms like this are still used around the world.

DETECTIVE WORK

Find out about Mayan weaving today at this website: http://www.jaguar-sun.com

'*Myth has it that Our Mother Moon, the goddess Ixchel, taught the first woman how to weave at the beginning of time. Since then, Maya mothers have taught their daughters, from generation to generation uninterruptedly for 3,000 years, how to wrap themselves around the loom and produce exquisite cloth.*'

Mayan Hands, a present-day cooperative of women weavers

▲ This terracotta figurine shows a Mayan woman weaving with a back-strap loom. Her ear flares and necklace show that she was of noble rank.

▶ People in Central America still weave using the same techniques as their ancestors. Perhaps ancient Mayan textiles were as bold and colourful as these modern blankets?

The Maya pierced their ears and put in heavy **ear flares** of jade or other precious stones. High-status men often had lip and nose plugs, too. Members of the elite showed off in shell pendants or necklaces and bracelets made of jade beads or jaguar fangs or claws. They even drilled holes into their teeth so they could decorate them with precious stones. Almost everyone filed their teeth to make them look more pointed, and wives sometimes dyed their teeth red with crushed cochineal beetles. After marriage, some men and woman also had tattoos, although this was a very painful process. First the design was painted on to the skin and then it was cut with a knife – the paint and scar combined to create the tattoo. Body paint was common and less severe. Warriors favoured patterns of black and red; priests painted themselves blue.

The Maya had surprising ideas of beauty: to look like the god of maize they wanted long heads and flowing hair. Parents pressed their newborn babies' heads into shape between boards. The Maya thought crossed eyes were attractive, too. Parents encouraged these by dangling an object in front of their child's nose! Finally, the Maya liked large, sloping noses. They stuffed objects into their nostrils to widen them.

Noblemen's headdresses were large and elaborate, jazzed up with jewels and feathers. By contrast, footwear was simple. People either wore sandals or went barefoot.

🐾 **Why did parents press their babies' heads between boards?**

WHAT ART DID THE MAYA MAKE?

Mayan art ranges from reliefs and sculptures to painted vases and murals. The Maya's intricately detailed books, called codices, were works of art, too. Artists were influenced by other Mesoamerican peoples, including the Olmecs, Teotihuacános and Toltecs.

Mayan sculptors carved tall stone slabs, or **stelae**, that depicted Mayan kings as divine beings. Copán has seven outstanding stelae, which were commissioned by King Uaxaclajuun Ub'aah Kawiil. The stonework of the most important Mayan buildings was often beautifully carved, especially the lintels (stone doorways), wall panels, altars or ball court hoops. Sculptors probably worked in wood as well, but very few examples survive. Artists also carved precious objects from jade, shell and bone. Stucco (plasterwork) was a popular medium for bust portraits. It could be moulded to make fine raised friezes on walls. Some of the oldest examples are at El Mirador and show human and animal figures, probably gods.

Stela B at Copán depicts Uaxaclajuun Ub'aah Kawiil, king from 695 to 738 CE and a great patron of the arts.

DETECTIVE WORK

This guide produced for junior visitors by the Washington Gallery of Art includes images of colourful figurines: http://www.nga.gov/kids/mayakids.pdf

Everyday pots were plain and ordinary, but Mayan ceramicists made fine vessels for ritual use. The Maya added ash, sand or rock rubble to the raw clay to strengthen it, then shaped it by hand. Once dry, the piece was inscribed, painted or decorated using slip, a watery form of clay that has been coloured with minerals. Although the Maya knew how to produce many different slips, they usually limited themselves to reds, creams and blacks. They used illustrations and hieroglyphs on their vases to tell mythological stories. Once the vessel had been decorated, it was fired.

Did Mayan potters use a potter's wheel?

Mayan painters covered the walls of palaces, temples, tombs and caves with striking **frescoes**. They produced larger-than-life scenes of divine and mythical creatures, battles, priests, nobles and entertainers. The frescoes in the Temple of the Murals at Bonampak fill three rooms and date from around 790 CE. The colours, achieved with mineral paints, are still vibrant today.

Standing 12 cm (4.8 in) tall, this vase shows a servant offering a container to a seated nobleman. Hieroglyphs help to tell the story.

Dr Bill Saturno discovered the oldest-known Mayan murals at San Bartolo:

'We found that three of the room's four walls were well preserved and that the ceilings were also in good shape in terms of the paintings on them, so we got an awful lot more than we bargained for.'

A procession of musicians adorns one of the walls in the temple at Bonampak. They are carrying rattles made from gourds.

WHAT DID MAYAN MERCHANTS TRADE?

The Maya were part of a large trading network. Merchants had their own god, Ek Chuah, who was usually shown with a bundle of goods on his back. They drove their human caravans along roads, down rivers and around the coasts in order to trade, often with fellow Maya but also with other Mesoamerican peoples.

The geography of the Mayan settlements was so varied that trade was essential – no city-state had all the resources necessary for everyday life. Some of the goods were basics; others were luxuries. Coastal Maya were rich in fish and salt but had no decent farmland so they needed to import maize and other produce. People along the coasts supplied conch shells which were used as trumpets, and stingray spines for bloodletting (see page 15). Flint and limestone were found in the lowland areas, while Maya in the northern highlands had access to valuable stones, including basalt, **obsidian** and jade. There was an important obsidian quarry in the southern highlands near Kaminaljuyu. The tropical lowlands were the place to find jaguar pelts, cacao beans and *pom* (**resin** that was burned as incense). The highland forests were a source of quetzal feathers.

Shells were traded for jewellery making. This pair of shell ear flares was found at Copán.

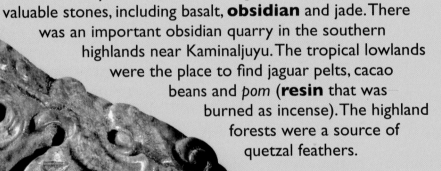

🐾 **What has been carved into the ear ornaments?**

Raw jade was in demand everywhere. Each city-state had its own craftworkers who specialized in carving it.

In addition to raw materials, the Maya traded commodities such as paper (produced from fig-tree bark), books, furniture, jewellery and textiles. The Maya did not really use money to buy and sell. Basic goods, such as foodstuffs, were simply **bartered** (swapped). Luxurious items were sometimes 'paid for' with valuable cacao beans, gold or jade.

When the Aztecs rose to power in central Mexico, the Maya exported feathers, jaguar skins and cacao to them in return for artefacts made of copper. It was easiest to access Aztec territory from along the coast, and Mayan merchants did this in wooden canoes 25 m (82 ft) long. Their own seaports included Isla Cerritos on the north coast of Yucatán, which served Chichén Itzá, and Tulum, which handled goods entering and leaving Cobá.

DETECTIVE WORK

Discover more about Mayan traders here: http://www.mayankids.com/mmkpeople/mksailing.htm

Anthony Andrews excavated the port of Isla Cerritos in the 1980s and investigated the likely route between the port and Chichén Itzá:

'The trade goods would have travelled on the backs of bearers, who could have walked the 100 km [62 mile] distance in from the coast in three days, with major rest stops at Panaba and Xuenkal.'

The Maya hunted resplendent quetzals in the rainforest and traded their dazzling green feathers with the Aztecs, whose emperors wore quetzal-feather headdresses.

WHAT HAPPENED TO THE MAYA?

Around 900 CE, many city-states in the southern lowlands were abandoned, but this was not the end of Mayan civilization. States in the uplands of the Yucatán peninsula continued to flourish until the arrival of the Spanish.

DETECTIVE WORK

For more information about the Maya, including a timeline, visit:
www.mayankids.com

One aspect of Chichén Itzá has had historians arguing for years. The city's architecture shares features with Tula, the Toltec capital. The Toltecs were a warlike people, and it is possible that they conquered Chichén Itzá at some point, but there is no record of this. It is just as likely that the Toltecs and Maya came into contact through trade, and adopted aspects of each other's culture. For example, Chichén Itzá is the only Mayan site with statues of the feathered serpent god Kukulcan, who was also worshipped by the Toltecs.

The Toltecs were not the only Mesoamericans rising in importance – the Aztecs would soon dominate central Mexico. They, too, traded with the Maya. Perhaps they would have eventually absorbed the last Mayan cities into their own empire? No one will ever know. Before that could happen, Spanish explorers reached Central America.

This reclining figure at Chichén Itzá is called a chacmool. It is a Toltec-influenced version of the Mayan rain god, Chac.

The first contact between the Maya and Europeans happened in 1502. By the 1540s the Spanish controlled almost all Mayan territory, although they did not conquer the last Mayan city (Tayasal in modern Guatemala) until 1697.

The Spanish forced the Maya to give up their own gods and become Christians. Father Diego de Landa arrived in the Yucatán in 1549 to help convert the Maya and was the region's bishop from 1573 to 1579. He was responsible for burning many Mayan books and figurines. The Spanish also – without meaning to – brought diseases that the Maya had no **immunity** against. The last city-states crumbled, but the people survived. Many headed into the forests to live again as slash-and-burn farmers, but some traded with the Europeans. Today, millions of the descendants of the Maya live across Central America. The legacy of their ancestors lives on in all the wonderful architecture and artefacts they left behind.

Guatemala and Mexico are home to most living Maya. This woman and her daughter are from Chiapas, Mexico.

UNESCO Goodwill Ambassador Rigoberta Menchú, who has campaigned for the rights of indigenous peoples in Guatemala, said in 1992:

'We are not myths of the past, ruins in the jungle or zoos. We are people and we want to be respected, not to be victims of intolerance and racism.'

What language does the word *cenote* come from?

The ancient Maya threw offerings into *cenotes* (underwater flooded caves). Today, these pools are a gateway to the past, where divers discover objects that tell us more about Mayan culture.

YOUR PROJECT

By now you should have collected lots of information about the Maya and their fascinating history. This is the time to think about the sort of project you might like to produce.

You might choose to make your own model pyramid. Have a look at examples from different sites and find a favourite to copy. Alternatively, you could make a poster showing interesting Mayan buildings from various city-states. Add a map, if you like, to show where they all are. Maybe you are fascinated by Mayan kings. Why not find as many images of Mayan rulers as you can, and then order them by date on to a timeline. See if you can write their names in glyphs. You might want to practise copying other Mayan writing.

You might wish to focus on ordinary life. Next time you visit the supermarket or vegetable market, note how many foods originally came from Central America. How would the Maya have eaten them? Look online for recipes and see if you can recreate any Mayan dishes.

You might have your own ideas for a project, but whatever you decide, remember it is your project, so choose something that interests you. Good luck!

Uxmal is dominated by the Pyramid of the Magician, which stands around 35 m (115 ft) tall.

Project presentation

- Do plenty of research before you begin. Use the Internet and your local or school library. Scan the television guide so you do not miss specialist programmes about Mayan sites.

- Collect as many pictures as you can to illustrate your project. Print off images from the Internet or make sketches from photographs. Buy postcards from museums if you can.

- If you were a news reporter and could travel back in time, what questions would you ask? Make a list and then see if you can answer them yourself through your research.

Images of Mayan kings appear in relief carvings, on vases and as busts. This bust shows Palenque's ruler, Pakal the Great.

Two columns of Mayan hieroglyphs cover the back of this jade plaque, which dates to the 400s CE.

GLOSSARY

administrator Someone who helps to run something, for example a city-state.

archaeologist Someone who studies the remains of past societies.

astronomer Someone who studies the planets, stars and universe.

bartered Traded by swapping goods, rather than using money.

BCE 'Before Common Era'. Used to signify years before the believed birth of Jesus, around 2,000 years ago.

bloodletting A ritual that involves deliberately shedding a person's blood.

caravan A long line of people or animals travelling in single file.

CE 'Common Era'. Used to signify years since the believed birth of Jesus.

city-state A self-governing, independent state consisting of a city and the surrounding area.

codex (plural codices) An ancient manuscript that makes up a book of writings.

dynasty A ruling family.

ear flare A large, circular ear ornament, inserted into the pierced lobe of the ear and often made of jade.

elite In Mayan society, the superior class of people that were second in importance only to the king.

fresco A painting on a freshly plastered wall.

hieroglyph A symbol used to represent a word or sound.

hunter-gatherer Someone who lives by hunting, fishing and collecting wild foods.

immunity The ability to resist a particular disease.

lintel A stone block that forms the top of a doorway. In Mayan architecture, lintels were intricately carved.

Mesoamerica The name for Central America and the civilizations that existed there before the arrival of the Spanish in the 1500s.

obsidian A glassy rock formed when volcanic lava cools.

pyramid A monument with a square base and sloping sides that meet at a point at the top.

quetzal Short for resplendent quetzal. A tropical bird native to Central America, prized for its colourful green tail feathers.

relief A carving that stands out or is raised from the surface.

resin A sticky, sometimes fragrant substance produced by trees.

slash-and-burn A way of clearing farmland, by slashing away most vegetation, then burning the rest.

stela (plural stelae) A tall, carved monumental stone.

warp string One of the strings arranged lengthways on a loom, between which the yarn is woven.

ANSWERS

Page 5: The king is wearing an ear flare (or ear plug) – a sign of status.

Page 7: The Maya ate farmed turkey or dog meat, or game such as venison, peccary or tapir.

Page 8: Bird Jaguar holds a spear, while his captive holds a broken parasol, a symbol of defeat.

Page 10: Pakal's mask is carved from precious jade.

Page 13: Beneath the priest's feet is a turtle shell, and under that is a human figure whom experts identify as god of the underworld.

Page 15: Her name is Lady K'ab'al Xook and she is pulling a thorn-covered rope through her tongue to make it bleed.

Page 17: Itzamna is holding a vision serpent – a sacred, bearded snake that allowed people to communicate with their ancestors or the gods.

Page 18: In the bottom left section the feathered serpent god Quetzalcoatl is carrying an axe. He can also be seen in the central section, ferrying a woman.

Page 21: Parents wanted to lengthen their children's heads while the skull bones were still soft.

Page 23: Mayan potters did not use a potter's wheel – they shaped the clay by hand.

Page 24: They show a face in profile. Experts know it is the face of a Mayan ruler.

Page 27: *Cenote* is Spanish, the national language in the countries that were once Mayan territory. However, some native peoples have kept alive the languages of their Mayan ancestors.

FURTHER INFORMATION

Books to read

Ancient Maya (National Geographic Investigates) by Nathaniel Harris (National Geographic Society, 2008)

The Ancient Maya by Lila Perl (Scholastic, 2005)

Aztec, Inca & Maya (Eyewitness) by Elizabeth Baquedano and Michel Zabe (Dorling Kindersley, 2011)

Tikal (Wonders of the World) by Elizabeth Mann (Mikaya Press, 2002)

Websites

http://maya.nmai.si.edu

http://mayaruins.com

http://www.jaguarstones.com/Maya.html

Note to parents and teachers: Every effort has been made by the publishers to ensure that these websites are suitable for children. However, because of the nature of the Internet, it is impossible to guarantee that the contents of these sites will not be altered. We strongly advise that Internet access is supervised by a responsible adult.

Places to visit

British Museum, London WC1B 3DG

National Museum of Anthropology, Mexico City, Mexico

National Museum of Archaeology and Ethnology, Guatemala City, Guatemala

Peabody Museum, Harvard, USA

INDEX

THE HISTORY DETECTIVE INVESTIGATES

Contents of all the titles in the series: